To The Castle!
A Kid's Guide To Helsingør, Denmark

Photography by John D. Weigand
Poetry by Penelope Dyan

Bellissima Publishing, LLC
Jamul, California
www.bellissimapublishing.com

Copyright © 2014 by Penny D. Weigand and John D. Weigand

All rights reserved. No part of this book may be
reproduced or transmitted in any form or by any means,
electronic or mechanical, including photocopying,
recording, or by any other means, or by any information or
storage retrieval system, without permission from the publisher.

.

ISBN 978-1-61477-199-9
First Edition

"To be, or not to be: that is the question . . ."

William Shakespeare's Hamlet
Act 3, Scene 1, line 1

To The Castle
Bellissima Publishing, LLC

Introduction

There is a wonderful castle, Kronborg Castle, that is a must see when you travel to Helsingør, Denmark; but there is something else that is very special in Helsingør that award winning author, attorney and former teacher, Penelope Dyan, and photographer John D. Weigand discovered along the way, a wonderful library, where a kid can have fun exploring hundreds of wonderful books, The Culture Yard – Centre For Knowledge - Children's Library! And yes, there are books written in English as well as Danish! Use this 'learn to read' book to practice your reading skills using word recognition, word repetition and rhyme, and see some of the sights in Helsingør, Denmark that author Penelope Dyan and photographer John D. Weignd saw!

And take note that the most interesting thing about Kronborg Castle is it was immortalized as 'Elsinore' in William Shakespeare's play, Hamlet; and it is one of the most important Renaissance castles in all of Northern Europe! It is also on UNESCO's World Heritage Sites List!

So have fun with reading and learning, and then watch the free music video on Bellissimavideo's YouTube channel that goes along with this book for even more learning fun!

To The Castle!
Bellissima Publishing, LLC

To The Castle!
A Kid's Guide To Helsingør, Denmark

Photography by John D. Weigand
Poetry by Penelope Dyan

Kronborg Castle sits on a hill,
surrounded by the mighty sea,
a stronghold built for a king,
as mighty as can be!
It is also the Castle Elsinore,
of William Shakespeare's play;
and the mere mention of it by this
writer of words (in Hamlet)
immortalized this castle
until this day!

This is a seafaring town,
as shown in this house of blue.
An artist must live here,
and perhaps a poet or two!
And do you think that
if you hopped aboard THAT boat,
upon THAT ocean you could float?

On the way to Kronborg castle,
there is a wonderful place,
filled with books galore.
You stop and take a look around,
and you find that this library*
has EVEN more!

*The Children's Library' at
'The Culture Yard – Centre For Knowledge'

Here you can sit upon a boat,
as though your imagination
you read, write, dream and float!

And you'll have to take TWO looks,
because even the Teddy bears
in THIS place have books!

You walk up to an old-time
rotary dial phone;
but it is NOT connected,
so you can't REALLY call home.
You'd like to talk to your BEST friend.
But all you can do right now is pretend.
And so you decide
to call your best friend twice,
because even pretending
to call your best friend is nice!

Then you find a comfortable spot,
so you grab some books,
and you read a lot!
Finally, your mom says,
"Come on, my dear;
because now it is time
to get out of here."
After all, it's Kronborg Castle
we came to see.
And it's getting late!
It's ALMOST three!"

And so you head up the hill,
and you arrive at the castle gate.
You squeal with delight
that you're NOT too late!
Dad says that you are acting wild.
Mom reminds your Dad
that you're STILL a child!

You walk, and you look all around.
You seem to cover a lot of ground!
There are colorful buildings.
The sky is blue.
Then Mom takes a good look at you.
You are getting tired.
You are dragging your feet.
She asks,
"Are you okay, my sweet?"

And just as you turn to go,
you see the castle cannons,
all set up in a row.
Then you shrug your shoulders,
because (after all)
nowhere in sight
is a SINGLE cannon ball!

You wonder if THIS anchor
once anchored a boat,
that upon the mighty seas did float.
You try to imagine it.
You close your eyes.
The boat must have been huge,
to use an anchor THIS size!

Finally, you walk through
the castle gate back door.
Mom says,
"Tomorrow we'll travel again!
and you'll see even MORE!"
Then, as ALL the things you have seen,
run right through your head,
Dad says that his FEET hurt,
and that HE is READY for BED!
Mom says impatiently,
"Just get over it.
We'll find a place soon
where you can sit!"

As you leave the castle grounds,
one thing seems to be
as true as true can be.
And that is that in Denmark,
all paths DO lead into the sea.
And as you look all around,
you imagine you hear
a mermaid's song.
Then Dad forgets all about
his tired feet,
and he complains that now
it is time to eat!
Mom says imagination fills the soul,
as Dad insists it's time to go!

"To know is nothing at all; to imagine is everything."

ALBERT EINSTEIN

www.ingramcontent.com/pod-product-compliance
Lightning Source LLC
LaVergne TN
LVHW071652060526
838200LV00029B/433